RISING STARS

FOOTBALL'S

NEW

WAVE

THE YOUNG SUPERSTARS
TAKING OVER THE GAME

WILL GRAVES

First Edition
First Printing, 2019

Book design by Sarah Taplin
Cover design by Sarah Taplin
Photographs ©: Damian Strohmeyer/AP Images, cover (center), 1 (center); Reed Hoffmann/AP Images, cover (left), 1 (left); Scott Boehm/AP Images, cover (right), 1 (right), back cover; Adam Hunger/AP Images, 4; Bill Kostroun/AP Images, 9; Jeff Roberson/AP Images, 12, 16; Jeff Haynes/Panini/AP Images, 20, 25; Mark J. Terrill/AP Images, 28; Marcio Jose Sanchez/AP Images, 33; Paul Sancya/AP Images, 36; Bruce Kluckhohn/AP Images, 42; Josie Lepe/AP Images, 44; Ben Margot/AP Images, 50, 99; Jack Dempsey/AP Images, 52; Michael Dwyer/AP Images, 58–59; David Richard/AP Images, 62; Carolyn Kaster/AP Images, 68; Mike McCarn/AP Images, 70; Mark LoMoglio/AP Images, 76; Lynne Sladky/AP Images, 78; Phelan M. Ebenhack/AP Images, 84; John Bazemore/AP Images, 86; Perry Knotts/AP Images, 92; Don Wright/AP Images, 94; Kevin Terrell/AP Images, 102; James D. Smith/AP Images, 108; Matt Patterson/AP Images, 110; Kirby Lee/AP Images, 114–115

Design Elements ©: Shutterstock

Press Box Books, an imprint of Press Room Editions.

Library of Congress Control Number: 2019937099

ISBN
978-1-63494-090-0 (paperback)
978-1-63494-091-7 (epub)
978-1-63494-092-4 (hosted ebook)

Distributed by North Star Editions, Inc.
2297 Waters Drive
Mendota Heights, MN 55120
www.northstareditions.com
Printed in the United States of America

TABLE OF CONTENTS

CHAPTER 1

SAQUON BARKLEY

Saquon Barkley took a look at the board that listed all the weightlifting records for Penn State running backs and thought to himself, "I know I can get all that."

Just a freshman at the time, Barkley wanted to make a strong first impression with the Nittany Lions. He knew the school had a long history of producing star running backs in the National Football League (NFL), from Pro Football Hall of Famer Franco Harris to former All-Pro Larry Johnson.

Barkley believed he could be next in the line.

"All those guys are amazing," Barkley said. "And I wanted to at least be mentioned in the same category as those guys."

Saquon Barkley barrels down the field for another first down for the New York Giants.

Barkley did more than that during his career with the Nittany Lions. He created a category all his own, both on the field and off.

The player who once worried he wouldn't be strong enough or fast enough proved he was plenty of both. His eye-popping workouts at Penn State became stuff of legend. He set a school record in the summer before his junior season when he took a bar with 405 pounds loaded on it and lifted it off the ground and over his head, leading some to label him an athletic "freak" (in a good way).

All those workouts came with a purpose far beyond just showcasing Barkley's strength. He firmly believed they would help him become one of the most dangerous and dynamic players in football.

He was right.

Barkley spent three years at Penn State, setting school records for touchdowns (53) and all-purpose yards (5,538) while finishing second in rushing yards (3,843) and developing a reputation as an electrifying playmaker.

"He's the best football player I've ever been around," Penn State coach James Franklin said.

Barkley opted to head to the NFL after his junior season. At the NFL combine, where players hoping to be drafted showcase their skills for scouts, Barkley put on a show. He bench-pressed 225 pounds 29 times. He ran the 40-yard dash in 4.40 seconds. And his 41-inch vertical leap is better than most National Basketball Association (NBA) players'.

Speed? Check. Power? Check. Athleticism? Check.

The only question about Barkley when the 2018 NFL Draft arrived centered on how high he would be taken. The Cleveland Browns had the top pick but were in serious need of a quarterback. The New York Giants had issues at quarterback, too, with two-time Super Bowl winner Eli Manning nearing the end of his career.

The Browns filled their quarterback need by taking Oklahoma's Baker Mayfield. But when the Giants were on the clock, they wouldn't resist bringing Barkley–who was born in New York City–home.

"At the end of the day, a great player is a great player," Giants general manager Dave Gettleman said. "He is a touchdown maker. He is a threat to take it to the house every time he gets his hands on the ball."

Barkley made an immediate impression on fans and his new teammates. He earned the nickname "SaQuads" Barkley because of the massive quadriceps muscles in his legs.

SIGNATURE MOVE

Every great running back seems to have a signature move. When Barkley is in trouble, his first instinct is to treat an opponent like an obstacle in "leapfrog." Barkley made a habit at Penn State of jumping over a would-be tackler much like a track star going over a hurdle on his way to the finish line. He discovered this talent during his freshman year at Penn State, when he soared over an Illinois defender for a touchdown.

"I took off at, like, the 4-yard line," Barkley said. "I was able to jump into the end zone. I would've gotten farther, but the guy kind of jumped up and hit me. After he hit me, my momentum just carried out, and it was kind of cool."

Barkley, however, stressed he doesn't want be known just for his high-flying antics.

"I don't want to be known as a hurdler," he said. "I'm not a hurdler. I'm a football player. I want to be known as a guy who breaks tackles; that's the whole objective of the game."

Barkley's incredible athleticism makes him difficult to stop.

"His quads are the size of my waist and whole upper body," Manning said. "I've never quite seen anything like it."

And the Giants have never seen anything quite like Barkley. He wasted little time proving he was more than just a workout phenom. In New York's

2018 preseason opener against Cleveland, he took a handoff from Manning and found his path blocked by a host of Browns. No biggie. Barkley shuffled his feet, slipped past a defender, and took off 39 yards down the sideline before being pushed out of bounds.

Barkley's play earned the respect of teammates and opponents alike.

"I think his first game, watching him, I was like, 'OK, this kid's got something,'" said seven-time Pro Bowl running back Adrian Peterson, who faced Barkley and the Giants twice in 2018 while playing for Washington. "Each time I see him I'm just like, 'OK, this guy can be really, really good.'"

Though New York struggled as a team in Barkley's rookie season, finishing 5–11, Barkley's play pointed to potentially better days ahead.

Barkley led the NFL in yards from scrimmage with 2,028, and his 1,307 rushing yards set a team rookie record.

"Getting 1,000 yards in the NFL is an amazing accomplishment, and being the first rookie ever for the Giants to do that is an even bigger one," Barkley said. "It's big because even though my name might go in the record book, it's not just myself. It's the offensive line play and the guys in the running back room. All those guys have been a tremendous help."

Barkley's teammates know he's simply being polite. His ability to turn a play that looks like it's going nowhere into a big gain isn't something that can be explained by good blocking or flashy weight-room accomplishments.

"I just know that you give him a couple of touches, he's going to make something big happen out of those couple of touches, so he's a player that's special," New York wide receiver Sterling Shepard said. "You got to give him the ball and he can make magic happen."

SAQUON BARKLEY AT-A-GLANCE

BIRTHPLACE: Bronx, New York
BIRTH DATE: February 9, 1997
POSITION: Running Back
SIZE: 5'11", 233 pounds
TEAM: New York Giants
COLLEGE: Penn State
DRAFTED: First round (No. 2 overall) in 2018

CHAPTER 2

STEFON DIGGS

"**B**uffalo Right" sounds like something you'd see on a highway sign while driving through Western New York. It's not.

The term is actually part of the Minnesota Vikings' playbook. It's now also etched into NFL lore thanks to the soft hands, steady feet, and quick thinking of wide receiver Stefon Diggs.

Following a dominant 2017 regular season, Diggs and the Vikings trailed the New Orleans Saints by a point with 10 seconds to go in the divisional round of the playoffs. Minnesota had no timeouts left and the ball at its 39-yard line, too far for any last-gasp field goal.

The Vikings needed a miracle.

Stefon Diggs goes up and grabs a last-ditch pass against the New Orleans Saints.

Diggs and Minnesota quarterback Case Keenum provided one.

Keenum called "Buffalo Right" in the huddle. As the Vikings moved toward the line of scrimmage, Keenum said, "I'm going to give somebody a shot" and looked over at Diggs.

Diggs sprinted off the line of scrimmage at the snap and headed toward the sideline. He figured the best chance—the only chance—the Vikings had of stealing the game would come if he could somehow catch the ball and get out of bounds to stop the clock with enough time for a lengthy field-goal attempt.

Fate had other plans.

Keenum spotted Diggs downfield and zipped the ball to him at the New Orleans 35. Five seconds were on the clock as Diggs leapt into the air to snag the pass. The sideline was two, maybe three steps away.

"My first thought was, 'Just let me try to get out of bounds, let me catch it,'" Diggs said. "I jumped in the air and paused to try to high-point the ball and prepare myself to get out of bounds."

It didn't look like Diggs would make it. New Orleans safety Marcus Williams was closing in fast. Williams dived at Diggs's feet, hoping to knock Diggs down and let the clock run out.

And then the weirdest thing happened. Williams missed Diggs, leaving him with the ball in his hands and nothing but open field in front of him. Diggs glanced at the Minnesota sideline. Should he just step out and set up the field goal? The look on the face of his coaches and teammates provided an emphatic answer.

No.

"In that split second I said, 'I'm going for the goal line. I'm taking it to the crib,'" Diggs said. "I looked inside to see if there was a defender near me, but I was clear."

So were the Vikings. Diggs raced the final 33 yards to the end zone for the game-winning touchdown. He held the ball out as he crossed the goal line and then extended his arms to the crowd in a mixture of joy and amazement.

"In the moment I was like, 'That's crazy,'" Diggs said. "I couldn't believe it. Nobody could believe it. It was so funny to see everybody's face. It was like, 'Did y'all just see what happened?'"

Diggs races into the end zone to complete the "Minneapolis Miracle."

The play, now known forever as the "Minneapolis Miracle," sent the Vikings to the National Football Conference (NFC) title game against the Philadelphia Eagles. It also stamped Diggs as a budding star, and an unlikely one at that.

The Vikings took a flyer on Diggs when they selected him in the fifth round of the 2015 draft. He had a productive college career at Maryland but didn't exactly stand out. He was fast, but not the fastest. He could jump, but not the highest. He was strong, but maybe not strong enough to hold his own with NFL cornerbacks.

Keenan McCardell, a former NFL receiver and Diggs's position coach at Maryland, promised scouts if they found a spot for Diggs, they would not be disappointed.

"I can tell you this—get the ball in his hands, and he's a different kind of football player," McCardell said.

McCardell was right in more ways than he knew. Diggs doesn't mind going against the grain. He grew up in the Washington, D.C., suburbs and was heavily recruited coming out of high school.

Yet rather than go to a powerhouse program, he decided to play for the Terrapins to remain close to his family, including younger brothers Trevon and Mar'Sean. All three boys were still recovering from the death of their father, Aron, at age 39 in 2008.

Before he passed, Aron asked Stefon to keep an eye on things.

"He just told me, 'Look after your brothers. Look after your mom. Look after your family,'" Stefon said. "That meant a lot to me."

Diggs ultimately did move away after the Vikings took him with the 146th overall pick. He knew making the roster was hardly guaranteed. So he poured himself into his work.

Diggs caught 52 passes as a rookie in 2015 and boosted that total to 84 in 2016 before his breakthrough in the 2017 playoffs. He hauled in 14 passes for 207 yards in Minnesota's two postseason games, including the 61-yard score that left little doubt about his speed, his smarts, or his strength.

A "HOMEBODY"

Though Diggs considers himself a "homebody," there's a bit of a thrill-seeker inside. Before he signed the $72 million contract in the summer of 2018, he went skydiving for the first time. It's just the way he approaches life in general.

"I don't know how to go halfway or do certain things in moderation," Diggs said. "You can't halfway bungee-jump. You can't halfway skydive. For me it's pushing myself and letting myself know there's nothing to be scared of."

The Vikings became believers, signing Diggs to a contract before the 2018 season that made him one of the highest-paid wideouts in the NFL.

Yet Diggs isn't content to just make a difference on the field. He works with local charities around Minneapolis. He hosts an annual turkey giveaway before Thanksgiving and makes regular appearances at area schools. His message is simple.

"I just tell them, 'Do what you feel. You can be anything you want to be in this life, with the right amount of effort,'" Diggs said. "Never let anybody tell you you can't do anything."

Diggs would know.

STEFON DIGGS AT-A-GLANCE

BIRTHPLACE: Gaithersburg, Maryland
BIRTH DATE: November 29, 1993
POSITION: Wide Receiver
SIZE: 6'0", 191 pounds
TEAM: Minnesota Vikings
COLLEGE: Maryland
DRAFTED: Fifth round (No. 146 overall) in 2015

CHAPTER 3

MYLES GARRETT

It's easy to explain Myles Garrett's love for playing football.

"I love to hit," he said.

All the time. Doesn't matter if it's minicamp or training camp. Practice or games. The Cleveland Browns defensive end wants you to know when his No. 95 is out there.

"I want to display a dominance when I'm on the field," Garrett said shortly after the Browns took him with the top pick in the 2017 draft. "So I'm trying to have a dominant performance, whether it's preseason first series or whenever I get out there."

Garrett plays with a swagger that provided the Browns a necessary jolt. Cleveland posted the worst record in the NFL (1–15) in 2016. The silver lining in a

Myles Garrett prepares to bust through the Jacksonville Jaguars' offensive line.

difficult season came the following spring. The Browns had the first overall pick in the draft and needs all over the board.

Yet when it came time for NFL Commissioner Roger Goodell to announce "The Cleveland Browns are on the clock" as the 2017 draft began, there was no drama. The team had long since made up its mind.

The Browns needed a player who could be a difference maker. Someone who would alter not just the outcome of games but the outcome of seasons. Someone who wouldn't be intimidated by the team's regrettable recent past.

Someone exactly like Garrett.

He was a two-time All-American during his college career at Texas A&M. Playing in the always tough Southeastern Conference (SEC), Garrett rolled up 31 sacks in three seasons before opting to skip his senior year and head for the NFL.

Garrett wowed scouts at the NFL combine, where he ran the 40-yard dash in 4.64 seconds, incredibly quick for someone 6-foot-4 and 272 pounds.

"He's a lot more powerful than people give him credit for," said New England Patriots offensive tackle Dan Skipper, who faced Garrett regularly while playing in college at Arkansas. "He's quick off the ball. He gets up the field, then he can come right into your chest and go through you."

Though the Browns were in serious need of a talent influx at several positions, including quarterback, they used the fourth No. 1 overall pick in franchise history on the 21-year-old with the big goals and the big mouth.

"He does not seem like a guy that's going to be either fazed by the limelight or success," said Sashi Brown, who served as Cleveland's general manager when the Browns selected Garrett. "Frankly, he is just a competitive kid that loves football. Wants to be the best. Wants to be the best at it. Maybe the best ever."

Garrett certainly has all the tools. He spent time with Hall of Fame defensive end Bruce Smith before the draft, and the Buffalo Bills legend could tell right away that Garrett could be something special.

"He's going to be successful," Smith said in the summer of 2017. "It's just the level of success that he reaches could be contingent upon the decisions that are made for him at an early stage of his career. The advice, the coaching, the tutelage that he gets right now could determine whether he's an impact player in his first or second year or his fourth or fifth year."

Injuries slowed Garrett early in his rookie season. A sprained ankle forced him to miss the first four games of 2017. But once he returned, he wasted little time in making an impact.

Garrett chased down New York Jets quarterback Josh McCown for a sack on his very first play as a professional. He added one more sack, in addition to two tackles for loss, in his NFL debut.

The Browns lost that game, however. They lost every other game in 2017, too, becoming just the second club ever to go 0–16.

Garrett, however, didn't let all the losing get him down. It made him angry, sure. It also made him work even harder to get the Browns back to respectability.

The team put together a video before the 2018 season that played off the opening credits of the TV comedy show *The Office*. In the video, Garrett takes a picture of Pittsburgh Steelers quarterback Ben Roethlisberger and places it in a shredder.

In the 2018 season opener, the video became reality. Garrett sacked Roethlisberger twice as the Browns rallied to a 21–21 tie, delivering on the promise

Garrett bursts off the line of scrimmage against the Kansas City Chiefs.

Garrett made on the night he was drafted. He said his first goal in the NFL was taking down Roethlisberger, a two-time Super Bowl winner.

Garrett didn't get his chance in 2017. He missed Cleveland's first game against the Steelers because he was hurt. Roethlisberger sat out the second meeting between the two teams to get ready for the playoffs. They were on the field together for the first time in Week 1 in 2018, and Garrett got his man.

"It was nice to finally meet and properly introduce myself before the game and during the game," Garrett said.

WRITING AND HITTING

As ferocious as Garrett can seem on the field, he's just as thoughtful off it. While not playing football, Garrett writes poetry. He says poetry helps him deal with the stresses that come with life.

"When you're a poet or reading poems, you feel every single word," Garrett said.

Garrett isn't shy about sharing his poems with the world. When NFL Films came to tape the Browns during 2018 training camp, he cracked open one of his books and let the crew film him as he wrote.

"I was a boy who liked to write long before I was a man who liked to hit people," Garrett said.

Garrett met plenty of other quarterbacks during his second season. He finished with 13.5 sacks in 2018, good enough for him to earn his first trip to the Pro Bowl. Even better? The Browns finished 7–8–1, a sign that brighter days are ahead, just as Garrett envisioned when he arrived.

Still, Garrett wasn't quite satisfied. He gave himself a "B-minus" for his play in 2018.

"It (was) a good year. It was not great," Garrett said. "It was not bad. Right there in the middle."

With nowhere to go—Garrett believes—but up.

MYLES GARRETT AT-A-GLANCE

BIRTHPLACE: Arlington, Texas
BIRTH DATE: December 29, 1993
POSITION: Defensive End
SIZE: 6'4", 272 pounds
TEAM: Cleveland Browns
COLLEGE: Texas A&M
DRAFTED: First round (No. 1 overall) in 2017

CHAPTER 4

JARED GOFF

It was just a birthday present, the kind fathers love giving to their sons as a way to teach them about the past. It didn't matter to Jerry Goff that Hall of Fame quarterback Joe Montana had long since retired, or that his son Jared was just turning four in that October of 1998.

Jared liked football, and if you lived in the San Francisco Bay area like the Goffs did, you rooted for the 49ers. And if you rooted for the 49ers, you needed to know about Montana, the quarterback nicknamed "Joe Cool" for his ability to thrive under pressure while leading the team to four Super Bowl championships between the 1981 and 1989 seasons.

So Jerry Goff happily gave Jared a 49ers jersey with Montana's iconic No. 16 on it on Jared's fourth birthday.

The Rams bet on Jared Goff to become one of the league's next superstar quarterbacks.

The number fit in more ways than one.

Like Montana, Goff grew up to be tall with blond hair, a strong and accurate arm, and quick feet. Like Montana, he was drafted by an NFL team in California looking to make a move in the right direction after years of losing.

Two weeks before the 2016 draft, the Los Angeles Rams pulled off a blockbuster trade with Tennessee to go from picking 15th to first. They wanted to make sure they landed the 6-foot-4, 222-pound player called "Mr. Perfect" during his standout college career at Cal.

The Rams were in the process of relocating to Los Angeles after spending more than two decades in St. Louis. They needed an exciting young player to get behind. They found him in the 21-year-old Goff.

"It feels like home," Goff said the day after being drafted. "I landed back in California, in sunny Southern California, and it feels like my home, and where I belong."

Even if it ended up taking a while for Goff to prove that he belonged. He sat on the bench for the majority of his rookie season while the Rams stuck with veteran Case Keenum. When Goff did play, he struggled. Los Angeles lost all seven of his starts in

2016. During a loss to the 49ers, Goff threw for just 90 yards and tossed a pair of interceptions.

Still, he tried to stay upbeat.

"I'm really trying to hope these (bad) days and these games will be ultimately good for us in the future, and I think they will be," Goff said. "I really think they will. I'm optimistic about them."

What Goff needed was a coach who believed in him. That coach arrived in January 2017 when the Rams turned to 30-year-old Sean McVay.

"I think it's really a fresh start for a lot of people," Goff said. "I think it's a really good feeling. "

TWO-SPORT STAR

Jared grew up playing both football and baseball. Jerry Goff was a catcher who spent a portion of six seasons in the major leagues. Jared thought about following in his father's footsteps and played shortstop on his high school team before deciding football was the way to go.

"He was good, but he had to work a lot harder to be successful," Jerry Goff said. "A lot more reps. Baseball is a game of failure. . . . And he'd get frustrated, whereas football came a little more naturally."

That freshness quickly turned the Rams from losers to winners and Goff from a project into a budding superstar. Goff's improvement from 2016 to 2017 was remarkable, like a student transforming a bad report card to straight A's.

The player who couldn't win a game as a rookie won 11 in his second season. He made the Pro Bowl after passing for 3,804 yards and 28 touchdowns against just seven interceptions. He limited mistakes. He loved going downfield for big plays—his 12.9 yards per completion led the entire NFL.

The Rams ended up losing in the first round of the 2017 playoffs, but a new day had arrived in Los Angeles.

"I think this organization is going in the right direction," McVay said.

And Goff was leading the way. While McVay and some of Goff's teammates—including All-Pro defensive tackle Aaron Donald and running back Todd Gurley—hogged the spotlight, the quarterback kept his head down and kept working.

The Rams entered the 2018 season with something they hadn't had in ages: high expectations. They somehow surpassed them thanks in large part to Goff.

He took another massive leap forward in his third season, throwing for 4,688 yards and 32 touchdowns

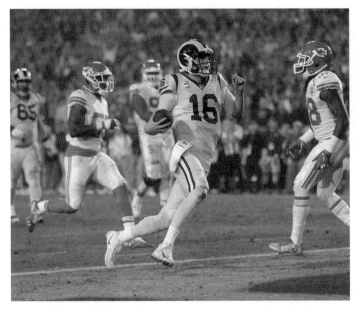

Goff runs into the end zone for a touchdown against the Kansas City Chiefs in 2018.

as the Rams went 13–3 to capture their second straight NFC West title.

Though Goff didn't always make headlines—even after tossing five touchdown passes in a victory over Minnesota or outdueling Kansas City quarterback Patrick Mahomes in a thrilling 54–51 win on *Monday Night Football*—opponents saw something special in Goff.

"That dude's a freaking monster," Los Angeles Chargers left tackle Russell Okung said. "And I

> **"THAT DUDE'S A FREAKING MONSTER. AND I THINK WHAT MAKES HIM A MONSTER IS HE'S INCREDIBLY CONSISTENT."**
>
> **—CHARGERS LEFT TACKLE RUSSELL OKUNG**

think what makes him a monster is he's incredibly consistent. Consistent players do the best in this league."

The Rams beat Dallas in the divisional round of the playoffs to reach the NFC Championship Game for the first time since the 2001 season.

Things looked bleak on the road against the New Orleans Saints. The crowd at the Superdome was typically rowdy, growing so loud that Goff had trouble hearing the play calls from the sideline as the Rams fell behind by 13 points.

The training staff came up with a solution: they put tape over the ear holes in Goff's helmet.

The noise cut down, Goff did something very Joe Montana–like.

He kept his cool and guided the Rams to victory. He passed for 297 yards and a touchdown, expertly putting together a two-minute drill to set up the tying field goal with 15 seconds left in regulation before Los Angeles won it in overtime.

"No matter what was going on, we looked to his face, and he was so calm and relaxed," Rams wide receiver Brandin Cooks said. "That's a special player."

Even if Goff's first trip to the Super Bowl wasn't quite so special. The Patriots shut down Goff and the rest of the Rams' high-powered offense, handing Los Angeles a 13–3 defeat.

Goff took responsibility for the setback, calling it the toughest loss he's ever had.

"It's a game I wish I would have played better," Goff said. "I wish I could have a million plays back."

The good news for the Rams and Goff? They have plenty of plays to look forward to.

JARED GOFF AT-A-GLANCE

BIRTHPLACE: Novato, California
BIRTH DATE: October 14, 1994
POSITION: Quarterback
SIZE: 6'4", 222 pounds
TEAM: Los Angeles Rams
COLLEGE: California
DRAFTED: First round (No. 1 overall) in 2016

CHAPTER 5

DANIELLE HUNTER

The sack that changed Danielle Hunter's life happened far away from the football field and without a quarterback in sight.

Hunter was born on the Caribbean island of Jamaica before moving to the United States when he was in elementary school. He didn't know a thing about the NFL when his family settled near Houston, Texas. He was playing tag with his friend Jamaal Holmes when he suddenly found himself "it."

So the nine-year-old Hunter did what every kid who is "it" does. He took off running. Hunter chased down Holmes in a flash—even though Holmes was on roller skates at the time.

A few feet away, Jerry Holmes—Jamaal's dad—watched Hunter close the gap on his son in awe.

Danielle Hunter is a force on the edge of the Minnesota Vikings' defensive line.

Holmes invited Hunter to join the youth football team he coached. And just like that, the career of one of the most ferocious pass rushers in the NFL was born.

"The first time I put on shoulder pads, I felt like I could run through a tree," Hunter said. "I felt invincible."

It's a feeling that Hunter kept close during his rapid rise from football newcomer to one of the most feared pass rushers in the NFL.

By the time Hunter was 17, he was playing for college football power Louisiana State (LSU). Though he picked up just 4½ sacks during his three seasons with the Tigers, Hunter was so confident in his abilities that he opted to declare for the NFL Draft rather than return for his senior season.

While teams were impressed with Hunter's 6-foot-5 frame, some experts thought he was crazy for turning pro.

"There is no doubt he's a physical specimen with considerable upside," NFL draft analyst Mike Mayock said before the 2015 draft. "But he was nowhere near ready to come out of LSU. He still has to learn how to play football."

The Minnesota Vikings saw things differently. Where some clubs saw Hunter as unpolished, the Vikings looked at Hunter and saw raw potential that could flourish in the right environment. Defensive line coach Andre Patterson knew Hunter was serious about proving he could play in the NFL shortly after Minnesota took him in the third round.

The two first met in Patterson's office, when the 20-year-old Hunter—at the time the youngest player

GATOR SANDWICH

Though Hunter never played football during his time in Jamaica, he and his friends still found interesting ways to pass the time. One day they played a game where they would roll down a hill toward an alligator pond. The goal was to get as close to the water as you could without going in . . . and potentially becoming lunch for one of the gators.

"I stopped at the last second, and I heard something swimming toward the land," Hunter said. "I got up as quick as I could and ran back up the hill."

It's the way a lot of NFL quarterbacks feel these days when they see Hunter on the other side of the line of scrimmage.

in the league—opened up his briefcase, took out a pad and paper, and started jotting down notes.

"By the time we were done, he had about 10 pages written," Patterson said.

It was symbolic of the way Hunter approaches his job. He knew when he arrived in Minnesota that he would have to soak in all the information he could if he wanted to get any playing time on a defense that was rounding into one of the league's best.

"There's a lot of people who just go out there when they come to the league, and they try to do their own stuff," Hunter said. "But I just sit down and I listen."

Hunter proved to be a quick study. He picked up six sacks as a rookie in 2015, using his quickness and long arms to swoop past offensive linemen on his way to the quarterback.

One team scout called Hunter "the freakiest athlete in the NFL." His teammates liken him to something out of a video game. He earned the tag "create a player" because of his unique combination of speed, strength, and smarts.

Hunter's sack total jumped to 12½ in his second season while he was still playing as a reserve. Vikings defensive tackle Linval Joseph invited Hunter to be his guest at the Pro Bowl at the end of the season. Joseph was sending Hunter a message: you're good enough to play in this game one day.

It didn't happen overnight. Hunter picked up just seven sacks in 2017 despite being elevated to starter. That didn't stop the Vikings from investing in Hunter. They awarded him a $72 million contract before the 2018 season. The deal included a $15 million signing bonus. How did Hunter celebrate? He flew right back to Houston to continue his rigorous offseason training program.

Hunter wasted little time making it appear like money well spent. He piled up 14½ sacks in 2018 to earn his first invitation to the Pro Bowl. In a victory over the Detroit Lions, he collected 3½ of Minnesota's team-record 10 sacks and added his second career touchdown on a fumble return.

> **"HE LOOKS LIKE A SUPERHERO. I EXPECTED THAT FROM HIM."**
>
> **–VIKINGS DEFENSIVE END EVERSON GRIFFEN**

"He looks like a superhero," said Vikings defensive end Everson Griffen. "I expected that from him."

Hunter wraps up San Francisco 49ers wide receiver Trent Taylor for a tackle in a 2018 game.

One who does his best to remain humble no matter how big his star gets.

"I don't think Danielle ever thinks that he's arrived," Minnesota coach Mike Zimmer said. "I think he's always trying to (say), 'What can I do better today?

What can I do better now? How am I going to get better?'"

Through 2018, Hunter had racked up 40 sacks, the second-most in team history for a player in his first four seasons with the team. Not bad for a player who didn't even know what a "sack" was before arriving in the United States.

Hunter, however, is quick to share the credit for his success.

"It's not me alone," he said. "I've got good teammates, a good defensive line again," Hunter said. "We go out there, and we work together as a team."

DANIELLE HUNTER AT-A-GLANCE

BIRTHPLACE: St. Catherine, Jamaica
BIRTH DATE: October 29, 1994
POSITION: Defensive End
SIZE: 6'5", 252 pounds
TEAM: Minnesota Vikings
COLLEGE: LSU
DRAFTED: Third round (No. 88 overall) in 2015

CHAPTER 6

GEORGE KITTLE

The Denver Broncos game-planned for George Kittle. The coaches worked on finding the right kind of coverages to keep the San Francisco 49ers' tight end in check ahead of their matchup late in the 2018 season. The players watched film over and over trying to get a read on Kittle, well aware their best shot at shutting down the 49ers hinged on shutting him down.

It didn't work. Not by a long shot.

Over the course of three hours on a sunny December afternoon, Kittle put on a show that not only carried the 49ers to a 20–14 victory but served notice that the former fifth-round draft pick was ready to be included in the conversation for the best player at his position.

With his big body and soft hands, George Kittle is a nightmare for defenders.

Catching seven passes for 210 yards and a touchdown in a half will do that. In the process, Kittle made a believer out of Broncos superstar linebacker Von Miller, who spent most of the first half futilely chasing after Kittle.

"There aren't too many tight ends in the league that can do that," Miller said. "We knew coming into the game that he was going to be talented, but the plays he made today, he just killed us. . . . He just killed us."

The Broncos were in good company.

Kittle got the best of just about everybody he faced in 2018. While the injury-ravaged 49ers managed just four wins in 2018, Kittle set an NFL record for receiving yards in one season by a tight end, hauling in 88 passes for 1,377 yards and five scores on his way to earning an invitation to the Pro Bowl.

Kittle, however, isn't one to keep track of his numbers.

"I just go out there and play football because I love it," Kittle said. "That is one thing that makes football pretty easy for me. If you love it and you enjoy it—when you're having a lot of fun—football is pretty easy. That is all I ever focused on."

Besides, catching passes is just part of the job description when you play tight end. You have to be an effective blocker, too. It can be a thankless proposition at times, one that requires more than just mashing the guy in front of you. Tight ends are often asked to take on a defender at the line of scrimmage, throw him to the side, and then get up the field looking for someone else to hit.

That kind of dirty work is something the 6-foot-4, 250-pound Kittle learned to embrace long ago. He didn't really have a choice. Not with a former offensive tackle as your dad.

Bruce Kittle starred in college for the Iowa Hawkeyes in the 1980s. By the time George was six, he was working on blocking drills with his father when he wasn't running pass routes against older sister Emma.

"I have probably thrown over 50 million deep balls to George on the sideline," Bruce Kittle said.

All those passes didn't go to waste.

George Kittle played college football at Iowa just like his pops, but opportunities to showcase what he could do were scarce for the run-heavy Hawkeyes. He caught just 48 passes in four seasons but showed a knack for getting into the end zone. He hauled in

10 touchdown passes over his final two years at Iowa, then impressed pro scouts by running a 4.52-second 40-yard dash at the NFL combine.

The 49ers saw enough to take Kittle in the fifth round of the 2017 draft and felt so confident in his development that they traded starting tight end Vance McDonald to Pittsburgh on the eve of Kittle's rookie season. San Francisco coach Kyle Shanahan was won over by Kittle's no-nonsense approach to his job.

"You can tell how he plays, that guy enjoys football," Shanahan said. "That's why he works the way he does. It's not to earn a contract or be famous. It's because

RUNS IN THE FAMILY

Kittle and his father are hardly the only accomplished athletes in the family. Older sister Emma played collegiate volleyball at Iowa and Oklahoma. His mother, Jan, is in the Iowa High School Sports Hall of Fame after starring in basketball and softball and later played college hoops at Drake. Kittle's cousin Jess Settles was the Big Ten Conference men's basketball Freshman of the Year at Iowa. Cousin Henry Krieger-Coble briefly played in the NFL. And another cousin, Brad Carlson, is the university's all-time leader in home runs.

he wants to be great at something he is passionate about, and you can see that in how he plays, how he is when the ball is in his hands."

Shanahan made it a point to make sure the ball gets in Kittle's hands frequently. Kittle brought in 43 passes for 515 yards in 2017, his numbers spiking after San Francisco traded for quarterback Jimmy Garoppolo.

"I think George is one of those guys that puts in a lot of extra work," Garoppolo said. "Whether it's staying after practice, talking in film sessions, he always asks me questions about his routes and stuff like that."

The 49ers hoped to take a big step forward as a team in 2018, but that plan went awry when Garoppolo was lost for the season due to a knee injury in Week 3.

> "I THINK GEORGE IS ONE OF THOSE GUYS THAT PUTS IN A LOT OF EXTRA WORK. WHETHER IT'S STAYING AFTER PRACTICE, TALKING IN FILM SESSIONS, HE ALWAYS ASKS ME QUESTIONS ABOUT HIS ROUTES AND STUFF LIKE THAT."
>
> —49ERS QUARTERBACK JIMMY GAROPPOLO

Kittle drags a New York Giants defender after making a catch in a 2018 game.

Though San Francisco struggled without him, Kittle did not. If anything, the 49ers relied more heavily on Kittle to take some of the pressure off backup quarterbacks C. J. Beathard and Nick Mullens.

Kittle responded by putting up one of the best seasons by any tight end in the history of the league. Four times he went over 100 yards receiving in a game in 2018. He could have toppled the record for most yards receiving by a tight end in a single game if the 49ers had looked his way in the second half of that victory over Denver. Kittle needed just five more yards to break the mark set by hall of famer Shannon Sharpe but didn't catch a pass over the final two quarters.

"George had one heck of a day," Mullens said. "Four yards short of the record. You can blame that on me, I guess."

Kittle didn't. Besides, at age 25 he figured to have plenty more chances to put his name all over the record book.

"We won," he said. "That's all that matters."

GEORGE KITTLE AT-A-GLANCE

BIRTHPLACE: Madison, Wisconsin
BIRTH DATE: October 9, 1993
POSITION: Tight End
SIZE: 6'4", 250 pounds
TEAM: San Francisco 49ers
COLLEGE: Iowa
DRAFTED: Fifth round (No. 146 overall) in 2017

CHAPTER 7

PATRICK MAHOMES

Patrick Mahomes took the snap and the play broke down in front of him, forcing the Kansas City Chiefs quarterback to scramble to his left as Denver Broncos linebacker Von Miller closed in.

As Miller attempted to wrap up Mahomes for a sack, Mahomes casually flicked a pass to teammate Tyreek Hill for a first down.

No big deal, right?

Then you check the replay and realize the right-handed Mahomes threw the ball with his left hand. He did it accurately, on time, on target, and with a shrug of his shoulders as if it was just something that came naturally.

"I saw it when it came out of his hand, and I went, 'Oh wow,'" fullback Anthony Sherman said after the

Patrick Mahomes passes with his left hand to secure another Kansas City Chiefs first down.

Chiefs rallied for a 27–23 victory in Week 4 of the 2018 season. "At this point, we should just trust him and know he won't put us in a bad situation. He'll find a way to get the ball to an open receiver."

Passing the ball with his non-dominant hand was one of many talents Mahomes showed off that year. The first-year starter was named the NFL's Most Valuable Player (MVP) for 2018 after throwing for 5,097 yards and 50 touchdowns. Mahomes said he was "humbled" by the honor, but maybe he shouldn't have been surprised. He's been leaving spectators wondering what they just saw seemingly from the first time he ever had a ball—be it a football or otherwise—in his hands.

The son of a former Major League Baseball (MLB) pitcher, Mahomes signed up for tee-ball when he was four. He was so far ahead of the other kids his age he ended up skipping tee-ball entirely and went straight to coach-pitch.

Mahomes was at shortstop during his first practice when he fielded a grounder and fired to first base. The throw came in so hard and so fast the first baseman didn't get his glove up in time. The ball ended up hitting the first baseman in the face, breaking his glasses.

It was the same when Mahomes started throwing a football. Playing in the backyard with his friends, he gunned a pass to his father.

"It felt like the nose of the football went through my hands," Pat Mahomes said.

The elder Mahomes was hardly the last person to marvel at his son's arm strength.

LIKE FATHER, LIKE SON

Growing up, it seemed Mahomes was going to follow in the footsteps of his father and one day pitch in the major leagues. With a fastball that reached 93 miles per hour, he struck out 16 batters while throwing a no-hitter in high school. Though he was told he would be a high pick in the MLB draft, Mahomes told teams he'd already made up his mind that he wanted to be a football player. The Detroit Tigers still took him in the 37th round of the 2014 draft, but by then Mahomes had his heart set on playing quarterback at Texas Tech.

"He clearly made a really good decision," said Tigers scout Tim Grieve.

Throughout his rise from high school prospect to a record-setting superstar at Texas Tech to NFL MVP following his wondrous first season as a starter in 2018, Mahomes has routinely inspired awe.

On his 68th and final throw during a workout for NFL scouts before the 2017 draft, he casually zipped a pass 80 yards into the tricky northern Texas wind.

"I have a big arm," Mahomes said. "Why not show it off?"

Kansas City Chiefs coach Andy Reid needed to see something more from Mahomes in the days leading up to the draft. So he brought Mahomes to Kansas City for an interview. Over the course of six hours, Reid tried to get a feel for how Mahomes would handle an NFL quarterback's average workday.

During a break for lunch, Reid walked by the office of Brett Veach, the team's co-director of player personnel at the time. Reid didn't say a word to Veach. Instead he just smiled and gave a thumbs-up.

"I remember coach looking at me like, 'Yeah, this is the dude,'" said Veach, who would later become the team's general manager.

So the Chiefs made an unusual move for a perennial playoff contender with an established quarterback on the roster in veteran Alex Smith: they traded up in the first round of the draft to grab Mahomes with the 10th overall pick.

"I think it's a great situation for this kid to come into," Reid said minutes after the selection.

For the Chiefs and Mahomes both.

Mahomes sat during his rookie season while Smith guided the Chiefs to another playoff berth. Mahomes made a spot start in the 2017 finale to give Smith a breather before the postseason, throwing for 284 yards in a victory over Denver.

It was all the Chiefs needed to know he was ready. They traded Smith to Washington a few months later and handed the keys to the franchise to Mahomes.

A star was born.

Mahomes threw for four touchdowns in the 2018 opener against the Los Angeles Chargers. A week later he finished with more scoring tosses (six) than incompletions (five) in a road win at Pittsburgh.

His 10 touchdown passes during the first two games set an NFL record and offered a sign of things to come.

"I see Pat doing this all season long," Chiefs tight end Travis Kelce said.

Mahomes throws for a touchdown in a 2018 game against the New England Patriots.

Kelce was right. The 23-year-old Mahomes became the youngest player to throw for 50 touchdowns in a season. He also became just the third quarterback,

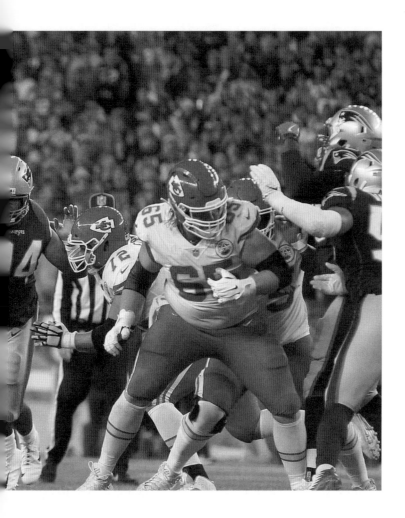

after legendary passers Tom Brady and Peyton Manning, to reach that milestone. And Mahomes was only just getting started in his NFL career.

Mahomes doesn't just rely on the strength of his right arm. His creativity allows him to come up with unusual ways to get out of tight spots.

If Mahomes isn't using his off-hand to get out of trouble—as he did against the Broncos—he's slinging it sidearm around defensive linemen or throwing a no-look pass like NBA star LeBron James, a trick he pulled out for a big gain against Baltimore in December.

Mahomes started messing around with a no-look throw in college. Still, his coach marveled at the confidence required to pull it off in an NFL game against the top-ranked defense in the league.

"Certain guys have vision," Reid said. "They can see. (Mahomes) does have real good vision. . . . I haven't seen a lot of guys do that."

Kansas City went 12–4 in 2018, winning the American Football Conference (AFC) West and locking up home-field advantage in the playoffs. After breezing by Indianapolis in the divisional round, the Chiefs hosted New England and star quarterback Brady in the AFC Championship.

The Chiefs fell behind by two touchdowns before rallying late to force overtime. Mahomes threw for 295 yards and three scores but could only watch from the sideline as Brady led the Patriots to the game-winning score on the first possession of the extra period.

Earlier in the season, the 41-year-old Brady called Mahomes the future of the NFL. After the championship game, Brady stopped by the Kansas City locker room afterward to congratulate Mahomes and offer some advice.

"(Brady) understands that time—it flies by, so put in the work," Mahomes said. "I think he saw that I put in the work to be in those situations."

For years to come.

PATRICK MAHOMES AT-A-GLANCE

BIRTHPLACE: Tyler, Texas
BIRTH DATE: September 17, 1995
POSITION: Quarterback
SIZE: 6'3", 230 pounds
TEAM: Kansas City Chiefs
COLLEGE: Texas Tech
DRAFTED: First round (No. 110 overall) in 2017

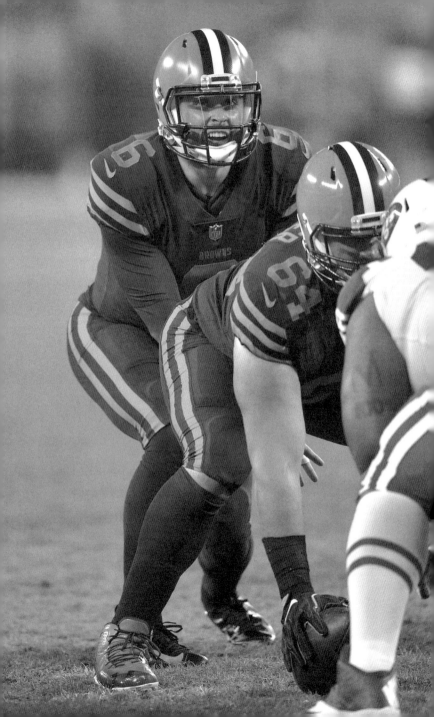

CHAPTER 8

BAKER MAYFIELD

Baker Mayfield's time had come. He knew it. The sellout crowd in Cleveland knew it. By the end of the night, the New York Jets and the rest of the NFL did, too.

The stadium erupted as Mayfield's No. 6 jersey appeared on the field in the first half against the New York Jets in Week 3 of the 2018 season.

Starting quarterback Tyrod Taylor had to leave the game with an injury. That's not why fans were excited, though. The woeful Browns—coming off the second 0–16 season in NFL history—had drafted Mayfield with the top pick in the 2018 draft and tasked him with helping the franchise shake free from two decades of losing.

Baker Mayfield's 2018 debut against the New York Jets signaled the beginning of a new era for the Browns.

The coaching staff, however, didn't want to rush Mayfield, who had won the 2017 Heisman Trophy while at Oklahoma. So Mayfield spent training camp and the early portion of his rookie season sitting behind Taylor, waiting for his chance.

Taylor's injury provided one. And just as he'd done throughout his remarkable rise from anonymous high school prospect to an NFL star, Mayfield didn't let his opportunity go to waste.

He connected with Jarvis Landry on his first NFL pass. His second was a 17-yard rope to tight end David Njoku. The Jets sacked him on the next play. No big deal. The player once considered too small to succeed in the pros dusted himself off and found Landry again to get the Browns within scoring range. Cleveland kicked a field goal just before the half.

It was the spark the Browns needed. Mayfield kept the momentum going in the second half. He finished the game with 201 passing yards and even caught a two-point conversion as the Browns rallied for a 21–17 victory. And it wasn't just any victory. It marked the Browns' first win since 2016.

Mayfield headed to the giddy Cleveland locker room afterward as the fans chanted his name. A new day had finally arrived at the home of the "Dawg Pound."

"As far back as when the Baker Mayfield story started, he has always made these types of plays," Landry said. "It's awesome to be a part of it."

While his teammates buzzed about his performance, Mayfield shrugged his shoulders. He'd won all of his life. Why should playing for Cleveland be any different?

"I have just been waiting for my moment," he said.

It's all Mayfield has ever needed. He officially took over as the starting quarterback on that muggy September night and led the Browns to a 7–8–1 record, their best in more than a decade. Mayfield finished with 27 touchdown passes, the most ever by a rookie quarterback in NFL history. His 3,725 passing yards set a rookie club record.

Yet Mayfield's influence goes far beyond his numbers. His confidence in himself and his teammates gave the Browns the jolt they needed to turn things around.

"We've got a quarterback who knows how to fight," defensive end Emmanuel Ogbah said. "You want to play for a guy like that who inspires you."

Maybe it's because Mayfield has made a lifelong habit out of proving doubters wrong. He put up eye-popping statistics during his high school career—the most important a 25-2 record as a starter. Yet, big-time colleges didn't come beating down his door. Most schools thought at just 6-foot-1, Mayfield was too short to succeed.

He enrolled at Texas Tech even though the Red Raiders didn't have a scholarship to offer him. Not that it mattered. Mayfield earned the starting job as a freshman walk-on, a rarity at any level of college football, let alone a team in one of the top conferences in the country.

Though Mayfield won each of his first five starts at Texas Tech, a knee injury cut short his season. He ended up leaving the Red Raiders after the season and enrolled at rival Oklahoma.

Again, he joined the team despite not having a scholarship. After sitting out a year due to college transfer rules, he won the starting job anyway.

Over the next three seasons Mayfield torched opposing defenses. He led Oklahoma to three straight Big 12 Conference titles and two appearances in the College Football Playoff. He easily captured the Heisman Trophy after his senior season in 2017.

Along the way Mayfield developed a reputation for playing with an edge—sometimes for better, sometimes for worse.

After the Sooners beat Ohio State on the road in early 2017, Mayfield took a flag with Oklahoma's logo on it and planted it at midfield, a move he apologized for. Later in the season he grew angry when Kansas players refused to shake hands at the opening coin toss and responded with a little trash talk and three touchdown passes in a 41–3 win.

PRO GAMER?

Mayfield's football career nearly ended before it really began thanks to video games.

Really.

Growing up in Austin, Texas, Mayfield would fire up his Xbox with his friends to pass the time. Their favorite game was *Halo*. Mayfield was good. Really good. So good that he considered cutting back on football and focusing on becoming a professional gamer.

Mayfield stuck with football but still plays in his downtime and has switched from *Halo* to *Fortnite*.

After several losing seasons in Cleveland, Mayfield gave fans a reason to believe in a brighter future.

Mayfield's sometimes brash behavior turned off some NFL teams. But not the Browns.

Cleveland had gone through a long list of quarterbacks since the city returned to the NFL in 1999. The Browns needed a player who could produce on the field and generate some buzz off it.

Mayfield checked both boxes resoundingly. When Cleveland general manager John Dorsey called Mayfield on the first night of the 2018 draft to tell him he was the top pick, Mayfield didn't boast. He cried.

"It just kind of brought out all of the emotions of the tough times that we went through, and the good ones," Mayfield said. "To think about it all there in that moment, it was going to be a fresh start."

One the Browns had been waiting decades for.

Mayfield joked after the Browns beat Atlanta in November 2018 that he woke up the morning of the game "feeling dangerous."

He might have been kidding, but his words hinted at a bigger truth. Cleveland, after years of missteps, is ready to win again.

"This team will follow him anywhere," Browns running back Nick Chubb said.

Good thing, because Mayfield is set on leading in his own unique way.

BAKER MAYFIELD AT-A-GLANCE

BIRTHPLACE: Austin, Texas
BIRTH DATE: April 14, 1995
POSITION: Quarterback
SIZE: 6'1", 215 pounds
TEAM: Cleveland Browns
COLLEGES: Texas Tech, Oklahoma
DRAFTED: First round (No. 1 overall) in 2018

CHAPTER 9

CHRISTIAN MCCAFFREY

Cam Newton expected Christian McCaffrey to turn toward the Carolina Panthers sideline and tap his helmet, football's universal sign for "Man, I'm tired. Coach, can I take a play or two off?"

Newton had just watched McCaffrey rip off a 59-yard run in the fourth quarter against Seattle in Week 12 of the 2018 season that put the Panthers deep in Seahawks territory. Newton assumed McCaffrey was gassed.

McCaffrey wasn't. For the versatile running back, getting tired is the only thing he doesn't do.

"When I'm in the game, there is so much adrenaline I never feel like I'm gasping," McCaffrey said. "You have to push through that."

Christian McCaffrey runs away from Seattle Seahawks defenders.

When the next play call came in—another run—Newton turned toward McCaffrey and asked if he was OK.

"He said, 'I'm ready to go,'" the Panthers quarterback recalled.

So McCaffrey got the ball again, and this time he ran for another 15 yards.

McCaffrey is always ready to go, even near the end of a draining afternoon in which he became the first player in Panthers history to go over 100 yards rushing and 100 yards receiving in the same game. McCaffrey finished with 125 yards on the ground and 112 yards receiving to pile up a franchise-record 237 all-purpose yards and two touchdowns.

The Panthers ended up losing 30–27, but McCaffrey's unstoppable performance drew praise from Seattle coach Pete Carroll.

"He's just a fantastic player," Carroll said. "It doesn't matter how big he is or how fast he is or whatever he is. He's just a great football player."

One determined not to be defined by his size.

McCaffrey doesn't quite fit the profile of the typical NFL running back. At 5-foot-11 and 205 pounds, he's not going to plow through defenders. He's fast but doesn't have true breakaway speed.

So what? McCaffrey makes up for it with the quickest feet in the league and hands so soft he could probably become one of the better wide receivers in the league if he felt like it.

McCaffrey finished 2018 with 1,098 rushing yards and 107 receptions, the most ever in a season by a running back. And he's just getting started.

"I love football," McCaffrey said. "As long as I'm playing, I'm always working to get better."

LIFE SAVER

McCaffrey's fast thinking isn't limited to the football field, and it ended up helping save Dan Smoker's life. McCaffrey was hiking a trail in Castle Rock, Colorado, in the spring of 2018 when Smoker lost his footing and fell in front of McCaffrey's group. Smoker was unconscious when McCaffrey's crew raced to help. McCaffrey called 911 emergency services while another hiker performed CPR.

Their efforts helped Smoker survive until paramedics arrived. He recovered, and McCaffrey later invited Smoker and his family to attend a Panthers game.

"I don't know what would have happened (if we weren't there)," McCaffrey said. "We were lucky to be at the right place at the right time."

It's one of the lessons passed down by his parents. McCaffrey's father, Ed, played 12 seasons at wide receiver in the NFL, winning three Super Bowls, including back-to-back titles with the Denver Broncos in 1997 and 1998.

Christian McCaffrey grew up around the game. When he was in middle school, his father figured his son could be on the way to stardom.

"When he got to about seventh grade and I couldn't catch him in the backyard, (I thought), 'You know what, he might have a little something,'" Ed McCaffrey said.

Or a lot of something.

McCaffrey played collegiately at Stanford, where he set records and left teammates, coaches, and opponents alike trying to find the right way to describe his talent.

Stanford coach David Shaw called McCaffrey "one of the best players that ever played college football." Peeking at the numbers, Shaw might have a point.

McCaffrey set a Football Bowl Subdivision record during his sophomore season at Stanford in 2015 when he piled up 3,864 all-purpose yards, smashing the mark held by Hall of Fame running back Barry Sanders. Shaw likened McCaffrey to a "Swiss Army knife," someone who could not just do a lot of things, but "do it extremely well."

Still, McCaffrey felt he needed to prove himself ahead of the 2017 NFL Draft. Sure, his statistics were remarkable. Yet McCaffrey knew that because there hadn't been many successful white quarterbacks in recent years, some people were overlooking him.

"I feel like a lot of people don't give me credit for my skills and talents," McCaffrey said. "That's just the way it is. But I also don't really care too much. I don't feel like I'm crazy disrespected. I play with a chip on my shoulder at all times. That's been my whole life."

The Panthers saw enough to take McCaffrey with the eighth overall pick in the 2017 draft, believing that his skill set would make him a perfect fit to play alongside Newton.

McCaffrey's electricity was evident from the day he arrived for his first NFL training camp in 2017. Sometimes it even came at the expense of his new teammates. Linebacker Jeremy Cash was tossed from practice for diving at McCaffrey's knees, a no-no because of the possibility of injury.

Cash went to coach Ron Rivera afterward with a startling admission. Cash wasn't trying to go low on

McCaffrey dives into the end zone for a touchdown against the Tampa Bay Buccaneers.

McCaffrey; it just kind of happened because Cash was caught flat-footed when McCaffrey faked Cash out of his cleats.

"I have never had a player tell me: 'Hey, coach, he shook me so bad that I fell into him,'" Rivera said.

Longtime Panthers running back Jonathan Stewart predicted "there's not going to be anyone in this league that can cover (McCaffrey) one on one."

Indeed, McCaffrey can be a matchup nightmare for defenses. Linebackers can't keep up with him, and he's strong enough to slip through the tackles of defensive backs. Even if you do everything right, McCaffrey can find ways to make you miss. McCaffrey credits his agility on hard work and a strict diet that keeps him away from dairy products, ice cream included.

Explaining what goes through his mind when he's on the field is a little tougher. If he's being honest, he's not sure how he does it. He just does.

"I don't think a whole lot as soon as the ball is in my hands," he said. "I kind of just try and feel everything out. Once you know where everybody's going, it can kind of slow down for you."

And speed up the path to stardom.

CHRISTIAN MCCAFFREY
AT-A-GLANCE

BIRTHPLACE: Castle Rock, Colorado
BIRTH DATE: June 7, 1996
POSITION: Running Back
SIZE: 5'11", 205 pounds
TEAM: Carolina Panthers
COLLEGE: Stanford
DRAFTED: First round (No. 8 overall) in 2017

CHAPTER 10

JALEN RAMSEY

Cornerback might be the toughest position in football. You're out there all alone near the sideline. You're standing across the line of scrimmage from a wide receiver who knows where he's going and knows that you don't. Behind the center there's a quarterback with a cannon for an arm waiting for you to make one mistake, no matter how small. Sprinkled all around you are officials who won't hesitate to throw a penalty flag if you put your hands in the wrong place at the wrong time.

Oh, and most of the time when the pass heads your way, you're going to fail.

To survive, you need a few things. Quick feet. Great instincts. Plenty of speed. A mind for the game. And, perhaps most important, a combination of supreme

Jalen Ramsey quickly established himself in the NFL as a shutdown cornerback.

confidence and an ability to quickly forget mistakes and move on to the next play.

In other words, you need to be Jalen Ramsey.

The NFL has a long history of "shutdown cornerbacks." Hall of famers such as Deion Sanders and Darrell Green would spend entire games shadowing the top receiver on the other team and finding a way to keep them in check, in effect "shutting them down."

Yet, as the league evolved, true shutdown corners became rare. New rules designed to help increase scoring made it more and more difficult for cornerbacks to do their job effectively.

By the time the Jacksonville Jaguars selected Ramsey with the fifth overall pick in the 2016 draft, playing cornerback seemed to be about as much fun as spending three hours in the dentist's chair every week.

Ramsey, however, has found a way to turn the tables. He doesn't think it's his job to deal with receivers. He thinks it's the receivers' job to deal with him.

Good luck to them.

During his first three seasons in the NFL, Ramsey became one of the league's top defensive players and one of its loudest talkers. The only thing in the league as fast as Ramsey's feet might be his mouth.

It's an approach he doesn't apologize for.

"To respect the game, you have to play it fierce," Ramsey said. "I don't believe in having friends on the field. I mean (if) my brother, my dad, my mom, grandma was out there, like, 'It's on. After the game we can be cool.'"

Ramsey's nonstop chatter works both ways. He does it in an attempt to rattle his opponents. He also does it because it forces him to play even harder.

THIS CORNER CAN CATCH

The old joke goes that the reason cornerbacks aren't wide receivers is because they can't catch. That's not the case with Ramsey. He showed off his pass-catching skills near the end of the 2018 season's Pro Bowl. With the AFC deep in NFC territory in the final minute, Ramsey checked in at wide receiver. He then caught a 6-yard touchdown pass from Houston Texans quarterback Deshaun Watson.

"I beg the Jaguars every week if I can get on the goal line," Ramsey said. "I know I can make some plays. Whatever I do, I can make plays. I hit them with a little quick move and Deshaun put the ball right on me."

"If I talk smack, I've got to back it up," Ramsey said.

That's something Ramsey has been doing practically since birth. He grew up outside Nashville, Tennessee, and spent his childhood trying to keep up with his brother Jamal, who is four years older. That meant playing games against bigger kids, ones who weren't interested in taking it easy on him.

"I had to have that confidence to keep up with them and hold my own," Ramsey said. "And then it just carried over into my life."

Developing into a massively talented athlete helped. Ramsey starred in both football and track throughout high school and college. He ran sprints and relays and was so good in the long jump that he briefly thought about trying to qualify for the 2016 Olympics.

"The Olympics, that's something that's always on my mind," Ramsey said in 2015. "It's definitely a real possibility."

The NFL ended up getting in the way.

Ramsey played three seasons at Florida State, becoming the first Seminoles cornerback to start as a freshman since Deion Sanders in the 1980s. He opted to go pro rather than return for his senior year, and the Jaguars practically sprinted to the podium to announce they'd taken Ramsey with their first-round pick.

Jacksonville general manager Dave Caldwell called the decision to take the 6-foot-1, 208-pound Ramsey "easy." It also turned out to be one of the few highlights for the franchise in 2016.

The Jaguars won just three games in Ramsey's rookie season. In the final moments of a loss to Detroit, Ramsey sat on the bench and cried in frustration. He wasn't used to losing.

Ramsey arrived at training camp in 2017 determined to help turn the Jaguars around. And just like that, it happened.

The Jaguars, led by the league's second best defense, captured the AFC South and reached the playoffs for the first time in a decade. Ramsey's evolution into one of the top cornerbacks in the NFL helped. He won over teammates, coaches, and opponents alike with his hard work both on the field and in the film room.

"What people don't necessarily see is how hard (he) works on the tape, in practice, how competitive he is in practice," Jaguars coach Doug Marrone said.

Ramsey intercepts a pass intended for Pittsburgh Steelers receiver Antonio Brown in 2018.

Though Ramsey's constant chatter can get under the skin of some receivers, he has earned the respect of others for the way he plays. Star receiver Antonio Brown called facing Ramsey something he looks forward to.

"Going against a guy like that makes it fun because you know that's going to be the measuring stick of where your level is at because you know that guy is at a high level," said Brown.

Ramsey was named an All-Pro for the first time in 2017, as the Jaguars made it to the AFC Championship Game. Ramsey boldly told fans Jacksonville would beat the New England Patriots and make their first trip to the Super Bowl. The Jaguars nearly did, taking a lead into the fourth quarter before the Patriots rallied to win. Ramsey didn't apologize for his prediction, even though it went bust.

"We're the AFC South champs, but that's all we are right now," Ramsey said. "We are not the AFC champs or the Super Bowl champs. We've got to work harder."

That has never been an issue for Ramsey. And though the Jaguars took a big step back in 2018, Ramsey reached the Pro Bowl for the second season in a row.

"It was a goal coming into the year to be the best I can," he said. "This is a step in the right direction."

JALEN RAMSEY AT-A-GLANCE

BIRTHPLACE: Smyrna, Tennessee
BIRTH DATE: October 24, 1994
POSITION: Cornerback
SIZE: 6'1", 208 pounds
TEAM: Jacksonville Jaguars
COLLEGE: Florida State
DRAFTED: First round (No. 5 overall) in 2016

CHAPTER 11

CALVIN RIDLEY

Every rookie wants to make a splash in his first season. Few do, mostly because adjusting to the speed of the NFL can be tricky.

Just not for Atlanta Falcons wide receiver Calvin Ridley.

The NFL has been around for a century. No pass catcher—not hall of famers Jerry Rice nor Randy Moss or current stars Antonio Brown or DeAndre Hopkins—in the history of the league put together the kind of start Ridley did in 2018.

Ridley scored six touchdowns during his first four games with the Falcons, the most ever by a rookie in the opening month of a season. He reached the end zone in a variety of ways. Bombs. Jump balls. Catch

Calvin Ridley began his career with the Atlanta Falcons in record-setting fashion.

and runs. He did it all with the finesse of a player who'd been in the NFL for years, not weeks.

The high point came in a loss to New Orleans in Week 3. Ridley caught seven passes from quarterback Matt Ryan for 146 yards, scoring on passes of 18, 75, and nine yards.

"He creates unbelievable separation," Ryan said. "His acceleration out of cuts is really good. His patience for a young receiver versus man-to-man coverage, knowing how to win and the timing of the play, all of that stuff usually takes a long time to learn, and he's been doing it naturally."

Ridley's always been fast. Yet he's well aware it takes more than pure speed to succeed in the NFL. It takes precise footwork and a complete knowledge of the offense. Not just where he's supposed to go, but where everyone else is supposed to go too.

When his coaches hand out the game plan for the next opponent, Ridley scribbles little notes to himself that outline the responsibility of every skill position player on a given snap.

"It could be 50 routes out there," Ridley said. "I'm going to write down every route. I write every concept out so I can learn them."

The mere act of writing it down helps Ridley absorb the information more efficiently. It's one of the reasons he made the transition from college to the pros look seamless, leaving some of his teammates to shake their head in awe.

"I'm surprised that (Ridley is) picking it up as fast as he is," said Falcons wide receiver Mohamed Sanu. "But I'm not surprised because of the amount of work he puts in. It's a great thing for him to be able to pick it up this fast and just keep growing and growing, because that's what we need. We need him."

HIGH FLYER

Ridley's leaping ability makes him one of the NFL's highest flyers. Yet it's not the only kind of flying he is interested in. Ridley would like to do some BASE jumping at some point. BASE jumpers leap from the top of a high structure—it could be a building or a bridge or a cliff—while wearing a parachute or a wingsuit.

"Everyone thinks I won't do it, and I definitely imagine it would be scary," Ridley said. "But I'm into wild stuff like that. And I'd wanna see everything. I'll keep my eyes open the whole way down and just ride."

Ridley doesn't believe he's doing anything out of the ordinary. If anything, he's simply trying to keep up with his mentor, Falcons star wide receiver Julio Jones.

Like Ridley, Jones was a college star at Alabama. Like Ridley, Jones was picked in the first round by the Atlanta Falcons. The two grew close when Ridley was still in school. Jones would return to Tuscaloosa, Alabama, to work out with some of the Crimson Tide during the offseason. So when the Falcons selected Ridley, Jones—a six-time Pro Bowl selection—took the rookie under his wing.

"He's like a coach," Ridley said. "He coaches me on everything. Even if I do it right, he's still going to coach me: 'You could do it better like this.' . . . So it's like having another coach on the field."

One with a serious interest in making sure Ridley capitalizes on his massive potential.

The two spend time together off the field, even going bowling occasionally. Jones believes he's doing for Ridley what former Atlanta wide receiver Roddy White did for him when Jones was a rookie in 2011.

Jones made it a point to try to eliminate the "distractions" that can pop up for first-year players, particularly ones who come in with high expectations like Ridley.

"I want him to go out and play well," Jones said. "Everybody doesn't need to talk to Calvin. He has it all. He just has to play."

That has never been a problem for Ridley, who's always been a step ahead. He was running by the time he was seven months old and became the top high school recruit in the country while playing for Monarch High School in Coconut Creek, Florida.

He cracked the starting lineup in his first season at Alabama and set a school record for a freshman by racking up 1,045 yards receiving.

He also became a not-so-secret weapon if things weren't going so well for the offense during practice. If the defensive players got a little too talkative, the offensive coaches had a simple solution to get them to pipe down: send Ridley long.

"Calvin would burn them deep almost every time," said Parker Barrineau, a college teammate of Ridley's. "That was (the coaches') best way to make the defense stop talking so much."

Ridley helped the Crimson Tide win two national titles in his three seasons at Alabama before heading

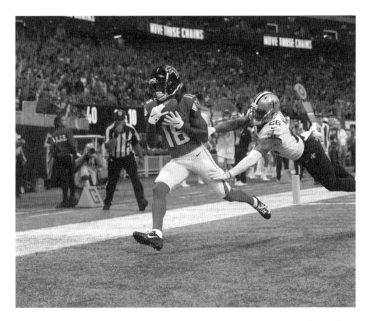

Ridley comes down with the ball for a touchdown against the New Orleans Saints.

to the NFL. He put up eye-popping numbers at the scouting combine, and the Falcons jumped at the chance to grab him when he was still available with the 26th overall pick.

Though Ridley was fired up to join the Falcons, a part of him wondered why it took so long for his name to be called. He was the second wide receiver taken in 2018, taken two picks behind D. J. Moore.

"I'm going to prove a lot of people wrong," Ridley said the night he was drafted. "I'm happy the Falcons selected me, but I could've been picked way before. I'm going to work hard and I'm going to prove everybody wrong who always doubted me. I'm going to make everybody believe."

Though Ridley cooled off a bit after his torrid start, he finished 2018 with 64 receptions for 821 yards and a franchise rookie record with 10 touchdowns. Impressive, to be sure, but Ridley and his teammates know he's just scratched the surface.

"He's a young player who has so much (room) to grow," Jones said. "He can do it. At the end of the day, (no one) can hold Cal back but Cal. He can be a great player in the league for a long time."

CALVIN RIDLEY AT-A-GLANCE

BIRTHPLACE: Fort Lauderdale, Florida
BIRTH DATE: December 20, 1994
POSITION: Wide Receiver
SIZE: 6'1", 190 pounds
TEAM: Atlanta Falcons
COLLEGE: Alabama
DRAFTED: First round (No. 26 overall) in 2018

CHAPTER 12

JUJU SMITH-SCHUSTER

Sure, making big-time catches is the dream—and the goal—of every NFL wide receiver. Yet there's more to the job than just sprinting down the field and leaping over a defensive back for a touchdown. Sometimes, wide receivers have to get their hands dirty in other ways.

That's where JuJu Smith-Schuster thrives.

The Pittsburgh Steelers' young star loves it when the ball is in his hands. His creative touchdown celebrations are LOL moments, whether he's playing hide-and-seek with his teammates or pretending to treat a football like a newborn baby.

There's more to Smith-Schuster's game, though, than just gaudy stats and giddy laughs.

JuJu Smith-Schuster hauls in a pass against the Baltimore Ravens.

There's an enthusiasm for crunching blocks that open holes for teammates and leave defenders lying on the ground wondering what hit them.

Just ask Minnesota Vikings safety Harrison Smith, who got an up-close look at Smith-Schuster's physical play in Week 2 of the 2017 season. Smith was closing in on Pittsburgh running back Le'Veon Bell when Smith-Schuster showed up and flattened Smith with one clean, but very hard, shot to the chest.

For a 20-year-old just a few months removed from college, Smith-Schuster's meeting with the All-Pro Smith sent a message to his teammates that he wasn't just some kid trying to learn the ropes.

"I think everybody has to show somebody something and what they're capable of," Smith-Schuster said. "When you have so many receivers that can do so many different things . . . I was huge on blocking in college. I just brought it here and showcased what I had."

Smith-Schuster's physical style of play is one of the reasons the Steelers selected him in the second round of the 2017 draft, making him the youngest player in the league.

Pittsburgh has always been drawn to receivers who embrace their inner offensive lineman. Hines Ward caught a franchise-record 1,000 passes and received a Super Bowl MVP Award during his 14 seasons with the Steelers. Yet it's his love of tussling with defenders that endeared him to teammates, coaches, and fans alike.

It's much the same for Smith-Schuster.

"Not only does he have the physical attributes to do it, he's got the mentality to do it, he's got the intelligence to do it," Pittsburgh coach Mike Tomlin said. "He's Hines Ward–like in some of those things. I

THE LONG HISTORY OF THE NAME

What's in a name? Quite a lot for Smith-Schuster.

He was named "John Smith" when he was born on November 22, 1996. His aunt started to call him "John John," but the nickname didn't stick. So she shortened it to "JuJu." It's the name Smith-Schuster prefers to be called, with one exception.

"If I want to be bothered, I use JuJu," he said. "If I don't want to be bothered, I say John."

As for his last name, Smith-Schuster added the "Schuster" after turning 18 to honor Lawrence Schuster, his stepfather, who helped raise him as a child.

realize what I said when I said that, but this guy enjoys it. He's embracing it, and I think it helps us."

Still, that's just one aspect of Smith-Schuster's game. Though he wasn't known as a true speedster during his college career at the University of Southern California (USC), Smith-Schuster quickly proved he's just as adept at running by defenders as he is running them over.

In a victory over Detroit in Week 8 of the 2017 season, he chased down a lob from quarterback Ben Roethlisberger and raced 97 yards for a touchdown, stiff-arming a pair of Lions defensive backs along the way. The play was the longest in franchise history. It also wasn't a fluke. In Week 12 of the 2018 season, Smith-Schuster did it again, turning a heave from Roethlisberger into another 97-yard score.

So much for Smith-Schuster not being fast enough to make it in the NFL.

"That was the biggest thing for me coming out of college, like 'He doesn't have breakaway speed, he doesn't have breakaway speed,'" Smith-Schuster said. "But it's like, 'C'mon.' You've seen what I've been doing."

Having a superstar on the other side of the field certainly helped. Smith-Schuster knows his rapid rise

Smith-Schuster makes a leaping catch against the Oakland Raiders.

from prospect to Pro Bowl selection—an honor he earned after hauling in a team-high 111 receptions in 2018—was due in large part to playing with superstar Antonio Brown.

Brown often drew double teams, meaning Smith-Schuster often had to beat only one man instead of two. Not that it stopped either of them much in 2018, when they became the sixth wide receiver duo in NFL history to each top 100 receptions in the same season. With Brown being traded prior to the 2019 season, however, Smith-Schuster is now in the starring role.

While Smith-Schuster takes his job very seriously, in many ways he's still a young player having the time of his life and only too happy to bring the rest of the world along for the ride.

He didn't have a driver's license when he moved to Pittsburgh. Growing up in Southern California, he didn't need one. So he spent a part of his rookie season making the short trip from his apartment to the Steelers' practice facility on his bike.

The fun ended, though, when Smith-Schuster's bike was stolen midway through his rookie season. When he posted the news on his Instagram page, the police got involved. The bike was recovered a short time later, and Smith-Schuster decided to have a little fun with it.

After scoring that record-setting touchdown against the Lions the following Sunday, Smith-Schuster went to the sideline, took out a chain and wrapped it around an exercise bike and waved his hands as if to say "no one takes my bike."

It was funny. It was also very, very JuJu.

A short time later, Smith-Schuster did earn his driver's license, thanks in part to being tutored by Steelers offensive lineman Alejandro Villanueva.

Underneath all that fun and all the laughs, however, is a player driven to be a difference-maker.

His teammates honored him in 2018 by naming him the Steelers' MVP.

"It means a lot that (my teammates) have my back," Smith-Schuster said.

Maybe it's because Smith-Schuster does such a good job of having theirs.

"I think most receivers are built to score touchdowns and make big plays," teammate Darrius Heyward-Bey said. "But every once in a while you've got a guy who's down to do it all, and JuJu's the perfect person. He doesn't know any better. He just wants to play football."

JUJU SMITH-SCHUSTER
AT-A-GLANCE

BIRTHPLACE: Long Beach, California
BIRTH DATE: November 22, 1996
POSITION: Wide Receiver
SIZE: 6'1", 215 pounds
TEAM: Pittsburgh Steelers
COLLEGE: USC
DRAFTED: Second round (No. 62 overall) in 2017

CHAPTER 13

LEIGHTON VANDER ESCH

Y ou don't need to see Leighton Vander Esch to know the Dallas Cowboys linebacker is fired up. Just close your eyes and listen for the howl.

Some players celebrate big plays by dancing or strutting. Vander Esch takes a different approach. He cups his hands around the front of his face mask and lets out his best wolf howl.

That's just the way the guy known as "The Wolf Hunter" rolls.

Vander Esch grew up in rural Riggins, Idaho, where his father, Darwin, owned an outfitting business. Vander Esch spent a large portion of his childhood hiking into the mountains, prepared to take on whatever crossed his path. On a 2017 trip to Alaska with his father—where Darwin also owned a hunting

Leighton Vander Esch lets out a howl during a January 2019 playoff game.

business—that included taking down a pair of gray wolves.

He showed the picture of himself posing with the wolves to the Dallas Cowboys coaching staff during a visit before the 2018 NFL Draft. The coaches immediately started referring to Vander Esch as "The Wolf Hunter."

It wasn't just his unusual hobby that made Vander Esch stand out. His raw athletic ability and his instincts for the game did, too.

He played both offense and defense at Salmon River High School, which played eight-man football because the school was so small. Though he helped Salmon River win two state championships, Vander Esch did not receive a single college scholarship offer after graduating.

Still, he always believed he could reach the NFL.

"From almost as early as I can remember, I was convinced that I was going to be a professional football player," Vander Esch said. "I was never not going to play in the NFL. I was bound and determined and serious about that."

Vander Esch walked on at Boise State. Though he'd grown to 6-foot-4, he still weighed just 200 pounds. Not exactly the kind of frame required to play linebacker in college football, let alone the NFL. His nickname during his early days at Boise State wasn't "The Wolf Hunter" but "Baby Giraffe."

The nickname didn't stick. By the time he was a junior, he was 256 pounds and lightning quick. He had the size to fend off offensive linemen and the speed to roam the entire width of the field to chase down opposing running backs and quarterbacks.

His coaches at Boise State believe Vander Esch's upbringing helped him transform quickly.

"I think growing up in the mountains has helped Leighton," Boise State coach Andy Avalos said. "It's taught him a lot about how to work and helping him develop."

Vander Esch did a little bit of everything during his junior season with the Broncos, finishing with 141 tackles, four sacks, and a pair of interceptions. He declared for the NFL Draft and wowed scouts and coaches at the combine.

The opening day of the 2018 draft, Vander Esch's phone rang as he sat backstage with other potential first-round picks. The Dallas Cowboys were on the line to tell him they were making him the 19th overall selection. And just like that, the kid from the mountains who had only 11 people in his high school graduating class was headed to the NFL.

Vander Esch called draft night "the craziest moment" of his life.

The craziness, however, faded quickly. Next came the hard part, the part that Vander Esch looked forward to: proving he was worth the risk.

"There's always pressure to perform," Vander Esch said. "Obviously, this is the biggest level now, so there's

THE VANDER ESCH EXPRESS

You'll always know when Vander Esch's family is at a Cowboys game. Darwin and Sandy Vander Esch have outfitted a custom-made bus they call "The Vander Esch Express." They purchased the bus when Leighton was playing at Boise State so they could make the trip from Riggins, Idaho, in comfort. The outside of the bus features a photo of Leighton with NFL Commissioner Roger Goodell the night Leighton was drafted.

It's become a popular destination for Cowboy fans—many of them wearing Leighton's No. 55 jersey—to stop by before home games at AT&T Stadium.

even more of it. You've just got to relax yourself and go out and do what you do."

What Vander Esch does, perhaps as well as any young linebacker in the league, is work. By the end of his first training camp, Vander Esch was in a rotation with the starters. By the end of September, he was starting in place of injured veteran Sean Lee, finishing with six tackles in a victory over the Detroit Lions.

"He balled," Cowboys defensive lineman Tyrone Crawford said. "I told him after the game, 'Man, keep it up. You're going to be great.' I truly believe that."

So does Vander Esch.

"There's a reason they drafted me in the first round, and I have to live up to that, so when they need me, I'm going to be there," he said.

Vander Esch might as well have said "everywhere."

Dallas stumbled early in 2018. The Cowboys were just 3–5 at midseason. Things started to turn, however, in November, and Vander Esch was right in the middle of the resurgence.

He racked up 13 tackles in a victory over the defending Super Bowl champion Philadelphia Eagles. Three weeks later, while facing the red-hot New Orleans Saints in a Thursday night game,

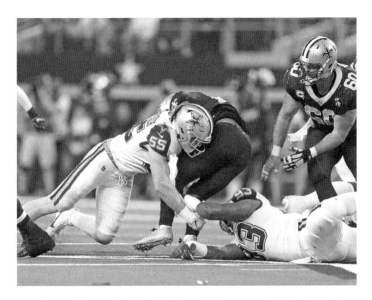

Vander Esch tackles New Orleans Saints running back Mark Ingram during their 2018 game.

"The Wolf Hunter" let loose. If he wasn't stuffing running backs for losses on third downs, he was harassing Saints quarterback Drew Brees.

"The Wolf Hunter" was on the loose. When Vander Esch let a howl rip after an important tackle to cut short a New Orleans drive, teammate Ezekiel Elliott felt "chills."

"The hairs on the back of my neck stood up," Elliott said.

Vander Esch's howls, his hits, and Cowboy victories kept piling up. Dallas won seven of its final eight games to finish 10–6 and win the NFC East title, then edged Seattle in the first round of the NFL playoffs.

The ride ended with a tough loss to the Los Angeles Rams in the divisional round. It was a difficult setback at the end of a season in which he earned a trip to the Pro Bowl after finishing with 140 tackles and tying for the team lead with two interceptions.

It was a great start for Vander Esch and the Cowboys. He's confident even better times lie ahead.

"The sky is the limit for us," Vander Esch said. "We got to keep building and making big jumps."

Big howls too.

LEIGHTON VANDER ESCH
AT-A-GLANCE

BIRTHPLACE: Riggins, Idaho
BIRTH DATE: February 8, 1996
POSITION: Linebacker
SIZE: 6'4", 256 pounds
TEAM: Dallas Cowboys
COLLEGE: Boise State
DRAFTED: First round (No. 19 overall) in 2018

CHAPTER 14

DESHAUN WATSON

What makes a great quarterback? NFL teams have been searching for the answer for a century. Is it a big body? A rocket arm? Fast feet? The ability to look across the line of scrimmage and immediately figure what the defense is doing? Is it a combination of all those things? Or is it something else entirely?

Enter Deshaun Watson.

At 6-foot-2 and 220 pounds, Watson is big, but not *that* big. His arm is strong, but not *that* strong. His feet are fast, but not *that* fast. He's smart, sure, but then again so are most quarterbacks who reach the NFL.

So what sets Watson apart? That's easy.

He wins. All the time. Doesn't matter if it's high school, college, or the NFL. When the clock reaches

Deshaun Watson led the Houston Texans to a division title in 2018, his first full season as a starter.

all zeroes, there's a good chance Watson and his teammates are on the right side of the final score.

It's why Dabo Swinney, Watson's college coach at Clemson, likened his star to basketball hall of famer Michael Jordan.

Swinney warned NFL teams that passed on Watson in the 2017 NFL Draft that it would be like saying you didn't want Jordan on your team. Lots of people laughed at the time, but Swinney didn't back down from his point.

"I'm just an old funky college coach, but Deshaun Watson is the best, by a long shot," Swinney said.

Swinney didn't need to look far for proof. Watson went 28–2 during his sophomore and junior seasons with the Tigers and led Clemson to the national title after the 2016 season.

All that winning and Watson's eye-popping stats, however, didn't exactly have NFL teams racing to draft him.

The Chicago Bears badly needed a quarterback in the 2017 draft and used the second overall pick on North Carolina's Mitchell Trubisky. The Kansas City Chiefs were set at quarterback with veteran Alex Smith but still moved up the draft board to take Patrick

Mahomes 10th overall. (OK, that one seems to have worked out—see Chapter 7.)

Sure, Trubisky and Mahomes were physical marvels. Yet their teams didn't win in college nearly as much as Watson won at Clemson.

The Texans, who had struggled for years to find a difference-maker at quarterback, saw in Watson what Swinney did. They traded up to 12th and happily selected Watson.

PLAYING FOR MOM

Watson didn't have to look far to find inspiration. He considers his mother, Deann, his hero. Deann battled cancer when Watson was growing up. She spent eight months in the hospital at one point, and Watson ended up working four jobs to help pay the bills, which he did in addition to going to school and playing high school football.

Deann ended up beating cancer. When Watson reached the NFL, he made it a point to make sure his mom was taken care of. During the 2018 season he helped renovate the family home in Gainesville, Georgia, so his mom would be more comfortable.

"Being a son and being able to take care of your momma and help her out felt good," he said.

Watson runs away from the Cincinnati Bengals on a 49-yard touchdown run.

"When the chips were down, he was able to lead his team to victory," Texans coach Bill O'Brien said on draft day. "And I think that says a lot about a quarterback.

In the end, one of the things that we always look at is, 'Is the guy a winner?' And this guy is a winner. . . . I don't think anyone can argue with that."

Still, the Texans intended to bring Watson along slowly. Veteran Tom Savage was ahead of him on the depth chart when he arrived at his first training camp. Houston wanted to give the young quarterback time to adjust to the NFL.

The plan lasted all of one half.

When Savage fumbled twice in the second quarter of the 2017 season opener against Jacksonville, O'Brien turned to Watson in the second half. The crowd roared when Watson ran onto the field. Though he couldn't orchestrate a comeback victory, his poise in his first taste of the NFL won over his teammates.

"That's what we needed, to go out there and get his feet wet," Houston star wide receiver DeAndre Hopkins said. "Even though the circumstances were what they were, I think he came in and went with the flow."

It's what Watson does.

O'Brien named Watson the starter the following week against Cincinnati. Watson arrived in style, wearing a tuxedo to the stadium.

Watson's clothes weren't the only thing slick about his first NFL start. He zig-zagged 49 yards for

Houston's only touchdown in a 13–9 win, wowing the Texans in the process.

"That's why he is who he is," defensive end Christian Covington said. "The whole sideline went crazy."

Watson did not. Others might have been surprised by his play. He wasn't.

"I don't get nervous when I step on the field," he said. "Football is football. This is what I've been dreaming of my whole life."

And what the Texans had long been dreaming of, too. For six giddy weeks in 2017, Watson offered proof that better days were ahead for Houston. He dueled with New England superstar Tom Brady. He went toe-to-toe with Seattle's Russell Wilson. He threw 18 touchdown passes over a five-week span and won AFC Offensive Player of the Month for October 2017. His arrival sent a clear message to Houston's rivals

> "I DON'T GET NERVOUS WHEN I STEP ON THE FIELD. FOOTBALL IS FOOTBALL. THIS IS WHAT I'VE BEEN DREAMING OF MY WHOLE LIFE."
>
> —DESHAUN WATSON

in the AFC South that they weren't dealing with the same old Texans anymore.

One bad step, however, cut Watson's rookie season short. He tore a ligament in his right knee during practice on November 2.

How did Watson respond to the injury that ended his breakout campaign? He went right back to work. He arrived at the stadium the day after getting hurt and asked Savage if he needed any help in preparing for that week's game against Indianapolis.

Watson refused to let the tough break get him down. He'd endured the same injury to his left knee during his freshman year at Clemson in 2014. He came back in 2015 better than ever.

It was much the same with the Texans. By the start of 2018, Watson was back under center, and after a bumpy 0–3 start Houston won 11 of its final 13 games to claim the AFC South title.

Watson did a little bit of everything. He became the first player in NFL history to throw for at

> "THE ORGANIZATION, (ITS) FUTURE, IT'S BRIGHT. HOPEFULLY, I'M A PART OF IT, FOR SURE, FOR A LONG TIME."
>
> —DESHAUN WATSON

least 4,000 yards and 25 touchdowns and add at least 500 yards and five touchdowns on the ground. He earned his first trip to the Pro Bowl in the process.

"The organization, (its) future, it's bright," Watson said. "Hopefully, I'm a part of it, for sure, for a long time."

If the Texans are interested in winning, that sounds like a brilliant idea.

DESHAUN WATSON AT-A-GLANCE

BIRTHPLACE: Gainesville, Georgia
BIRTH DATE: September 14, 1995
POSITION: Quarterback
SIZE: 6'2", 220 pounds
TEAM: Houston Texans
COLLEGE: Clemson
DRAFTED: First round (No. 12 overall) in 2017

ROOKIE RECORDS

MOST PASSING YARDS

1. Andrew Luck, Indianapolis Colts (2012): 4,374
2. Cam Newton, Carolina Panthers (2011): 4,051
3. Jameis Winston, Tampa Bay Buccaneers (2015): 4,042

MOST RUSHING YARDS

1. Eric Dickerson, Los Angeles Rams (1983): 1,808
2. George Rogers, New Orleans Saints (1981): 1,674
3. Ezekiel Elliott, Dallas Cowboys (2016): 1,631

MOST RECEPTIONS

1. Anquan Boldin, Arizona Cardinals (2003): 101
2. Michael Thomas, New Orleans Saints (2016): 92
3T. Eddie Royal, Denver Broncos (2008): 91
3T. Odell Beckham Jr., New York Giants (2014): 91
3T. Saquon Barkley, New York Giants (2018): 91

MOST SACKS

1. Jevon Kearse, Tennessee Titans (1999): 14.5
2. Aldon Smith, San Francisco 49ers (2011): 14.0
3. Dwight Freeney, Indianapolis Colts (2002): 13.0

Accurate through the 2018 season

NEW WAVE DREAM TEAM

What might a dream team of players born in 1995 or later look like? Here's what the author says.

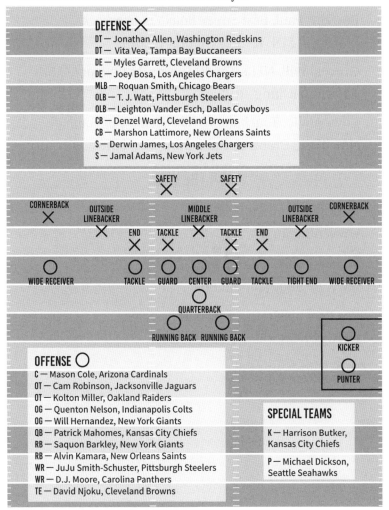

DEFENSE ✕
DT — Jonathan Allen, Washington Redskins
DT — Vita Vea, Tampa Bay Buccaneers
DE — Myles Garrett, Cleveland Browns
DE — Joey Bosa, Los Angeles Chargers
MLB — Roquan Smith, Chicago Bears
OLB — T. J. Watt, Pittsburgh Steelers
OLB — Leighton Vander Esch, Dallas Cowboys
CB — Denzel Ward, Cleveland Browns
CB — Marshon Lattimore, New Orleans Saints
S — Derwin James, Los Angeles Chargers
S — Jamal Adams, New York Jets

SAFETY ✕ SAFETY ✕

CORNERBACK ✕ OUTSIDE LINEBACKER MIDDLE LINEBACKER OUTSIDE LINEBACKER CORNERBACK ✕
✕ ✕
END ✕ TACKLE ✕ TACKLE ✕ END ✕

WIDE RECEIVER ○ TACKLE ○ GUARD ○ CENTER ○ GUARD ○ TACKLE ○ TIGHT END ○ WIDE RECEIVER ○

QUARTERBACK ○

RUNNING BACK ○ RUNNING BACK ○

KICKER ○

PUNTER ○

OFFENSE ○
C — Mason Cole, Arizona Cardinals
OT — Cam Robinson, Jacksonville Jaguars
OT — Kolton Miller, Oakland Raiders
OG — Quenton Nelson, Indianapolis Colts
OG — Will Hernandez, New York Giants
QB — Patrick Mahomes, Kansas City Chiefs
RB — Saquon Barkley, New York Giants
RB — Alvin Kamara, New Orleans Saints
WR — JuJu Smith-Schuster, Pittsburgh Steelers
WR — D.J. Moore, Carolina Panthers
TE — David Njoku, Cleveland Browns

SPECIAL TEAMS

K — Harrison Butker, Kansas City Chiefs

P — Michael Dickson, Seattle Seahawks

121

FOR MORE INFORMATION

BOOKS

Bowker, Paul. *Best Super Bowl Quarterbacks.* Mankato, MN: 12-Story Library, 2019.

Graves, Will. *NFL's Top 10 Upsets.* Minneapolis, MN: Abdo Publishing, 2018.

Kovacs, Vic. *Touchdown!: The History of Football.* New York: Crabtree Publishing Co., 2016.

ON THE WEB

National Football League
www.nfl.com

Pro Football Hall of Fame
www.profootballhof.com

Pro Football Reference
www.pro-football-reference.com

PLACES TO VISIT

Lambeau Field
1265 Lombardi Ave.
Green Bay, WI 54304
920-569-7500
www.packers.com/lambeau-field/

The home of the Green Bay Packers is one of the oldest stadiums in the NFL, having been built in 1957. It is also the site of the Packers Hall of Fame, which features exhibits surrounding the history of the franchise and the many great players who have worn green-and-gold.

Pro Football Hall of Fame
2121 George Halas Dr. NW
Canton, OH 44708
330-456-8207
www.profootballhof.com

The Hall of Fame is like a museum dedicated to football. There are exhibits on the origin of the game, artifacts from famous moments, and busts honoring the greatest players and coaches ever.

SELECT BIBLIOGRAPHY

Associated Press. "NFL sack leader Danielle Hunter 'just lets it rip' for Vikes." *USA Today*, 5 Nov. 2018, www.usatoday.com/story/sports/nfl/2018/11/05/nfl-sack-leader-danielle-hunter-just-lets-it-rip-for-vikes/38404343/.

Bittner, Adam. "How does the Antonio Brown/JuJu Smith-Schuster tandem stack up to other great duos?" *Pittsburgh Post-Gazette*, 3 Jan. 2019, www.post-gazette.com/sports/steelers/2019/01/03/antonio-brown-juju-smith-schuster-steelers-emmanuel-sanders-demaryius-thomas/stories/201901030069.

Cunningham, Kevin. "James Franklin on Saquon Barkley: 'I've been blessed to coach him.'" *Springfield News-Sun*, 23 Oct. 2017, www.springfieldnewssun.com/sports/college/james-franklin-saquon-barkley-been-blessed-coach-him/9CNn49omk3bg1XVoXtIWCL/.

Florio, Mike. "Deshaun Watson recovered from torn ACL in 2014." NBC *Sports*, 3 Nov. 2017, www.profootballtalk.nbcsports.com/2017/11/03/deshaun-watson-recovered-from-torn-acl-in-2014/.

Gorcey, Ryan. "Rams QB Jared Goff returns home to play his childhood team in a superlative season." *San Francisco Examiner*, 21 Oct. 2018, www.sfexaminer.com/sports/rams-qb-jared-goff-returns-home-to-play-his-childhood-team-in-a-superlative-season/.

Huguenin, Mike. "Florida State CB Jalen Ramsey has Olympic long jump dreams." NFL, 4 June 2015, http://fw.to/iX5unQY.

Rosenberg, Matt. "Steelers' JuJu Smith-Schuster's stolen bike found in Mt. Oliver, police said." *Trib Live*, 25 Oct. 2017, archive.triblive.com/sports/steelers/12874137-74/steelers-juju-smith-schusters-stolen-bike-found-in-mt-oliver-police-said.

Shalin, Mike. "What Tom Brady and Patrick Mahomes had to say about each other." *Boston.com*, 12 Oct. 2018, www.boston.com/sports/new-england-patriots/2018/10/12/tom-brady-patrick-mahomes-patriots-chiefs.

INDEX

ABOUT THE AUTHOR

Will Graves once dreamed of being a hotshot NFL wide receiver, but his playing career ended after a one-season stint as an offensive lineman and linebacker on the 75-pound Waldorf Wildcats in 1985. Instead of catching passes, Graves writes about the players who make them while covering the NFL and other sports for the Associated Press. An author of more than a dozen sports books, Graves lives in Pittsburgh with his wife and two children.